AF261525

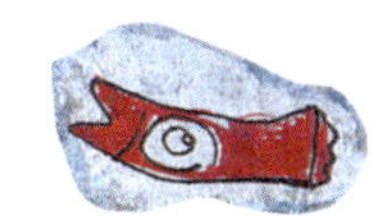
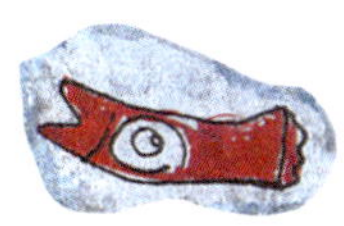
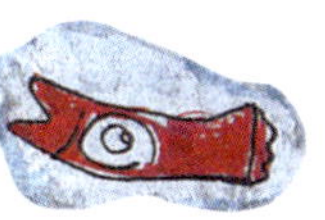
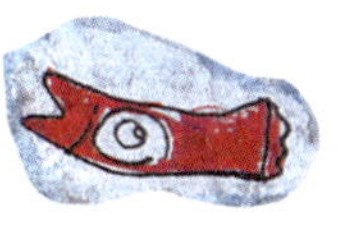
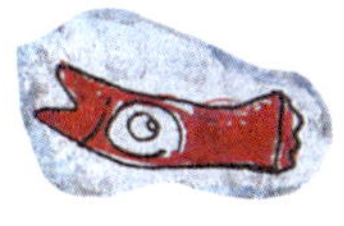
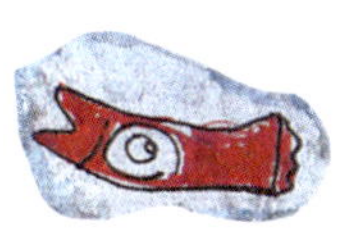
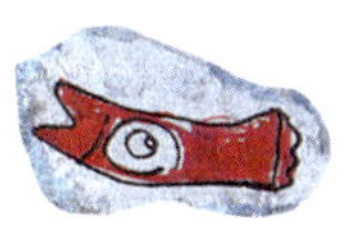
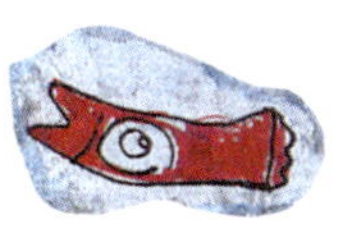

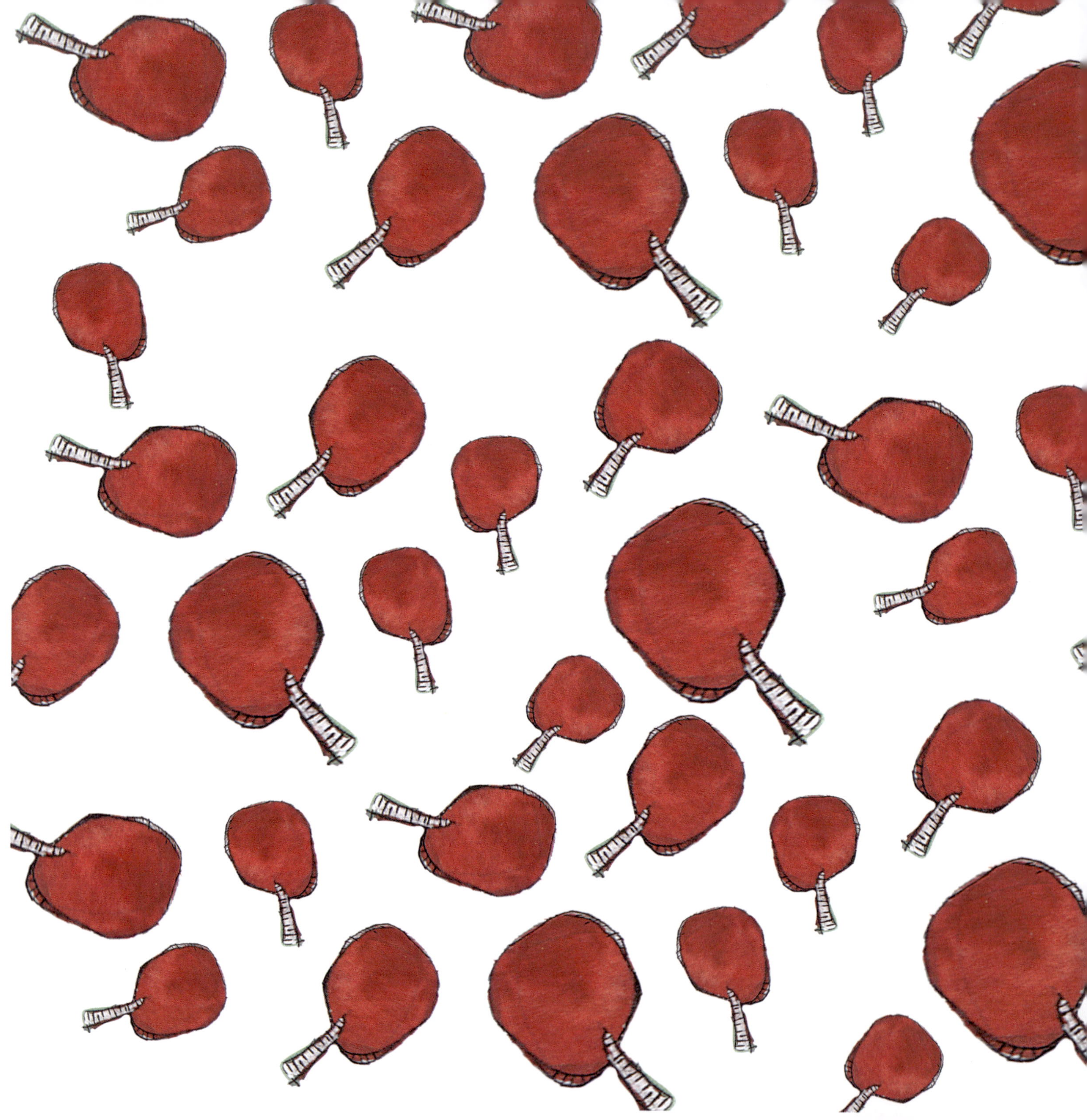

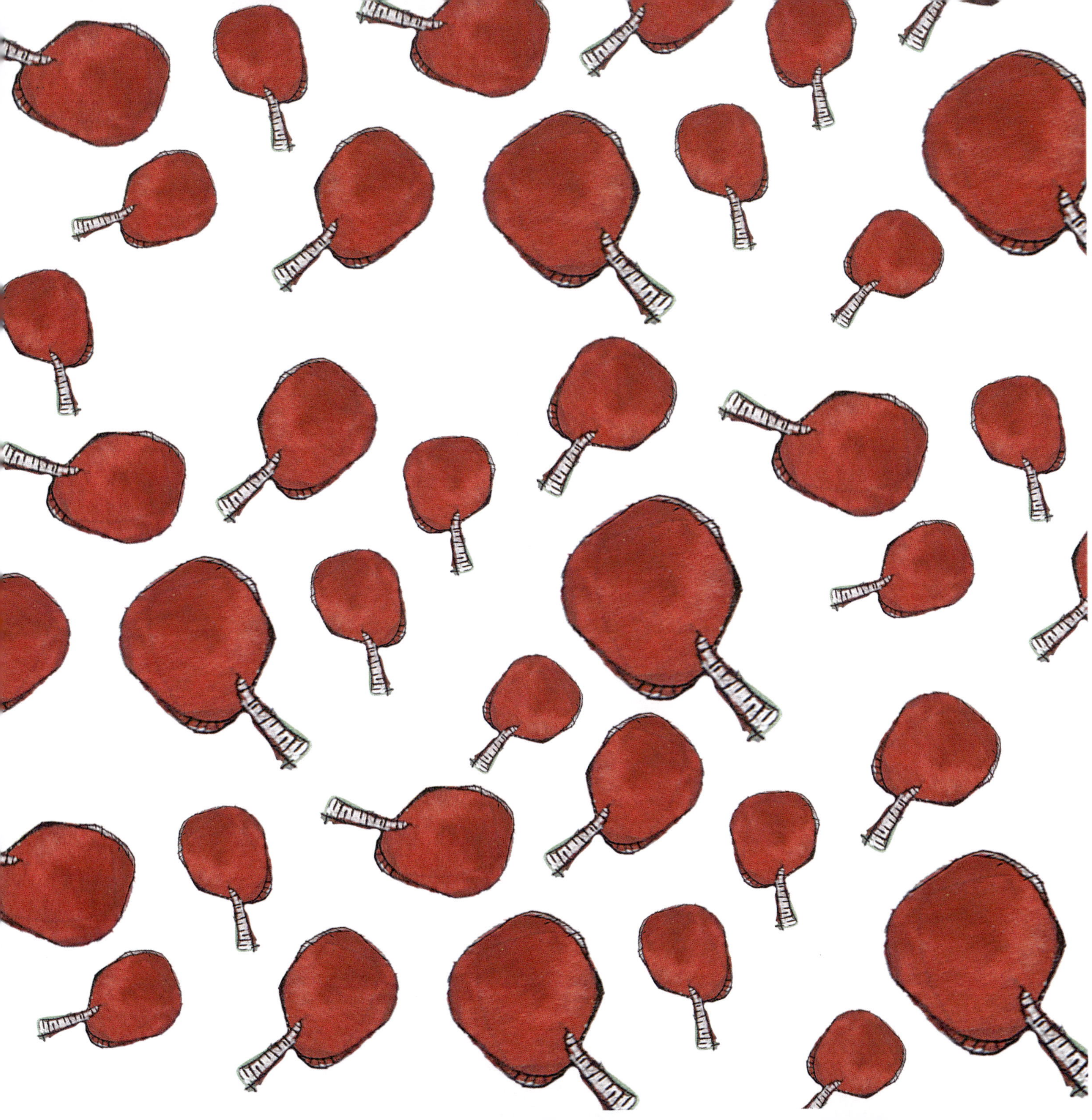

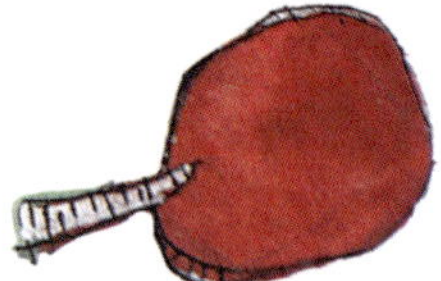

OLEASTER TREE

BAHAR TAGHIANI

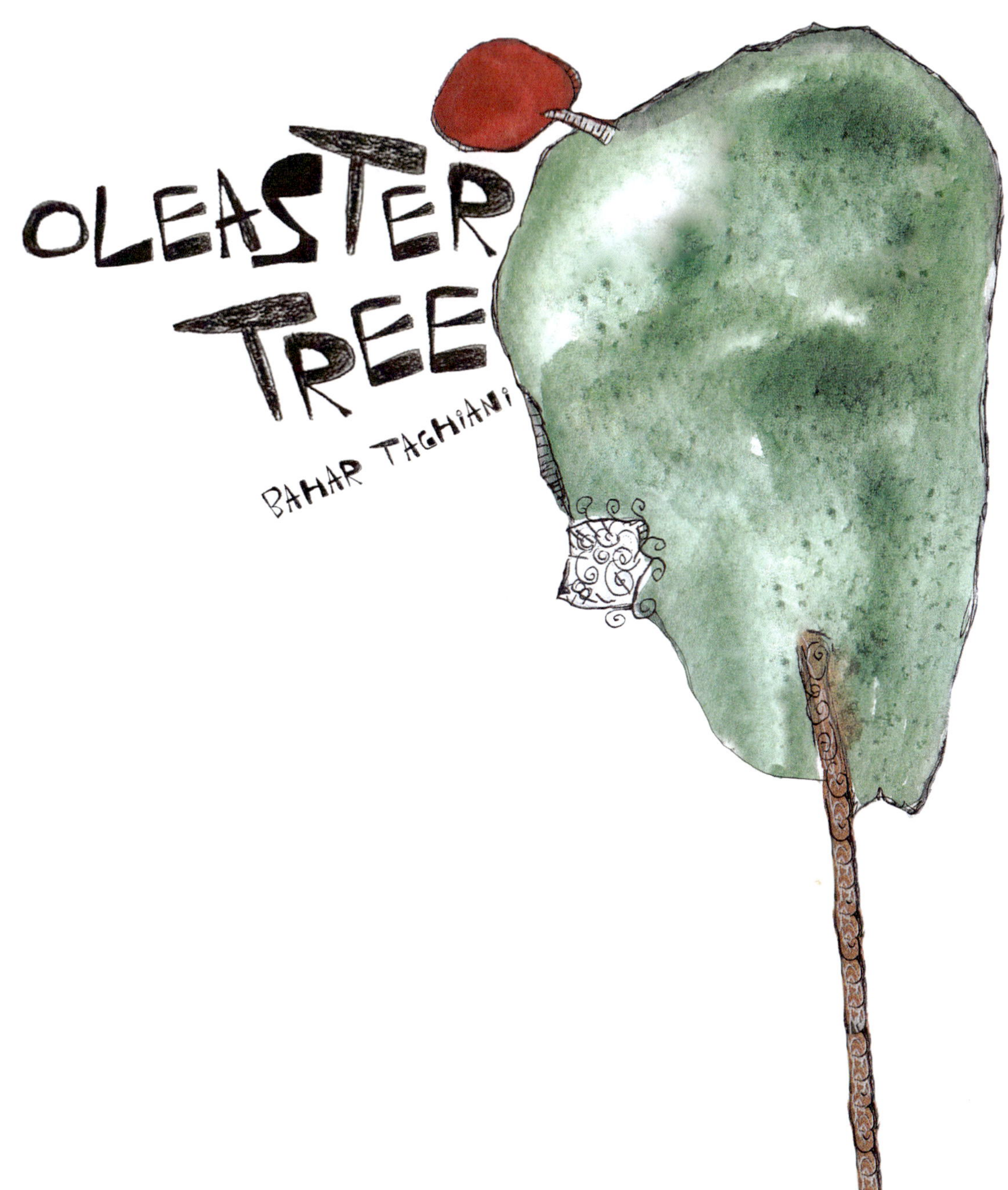

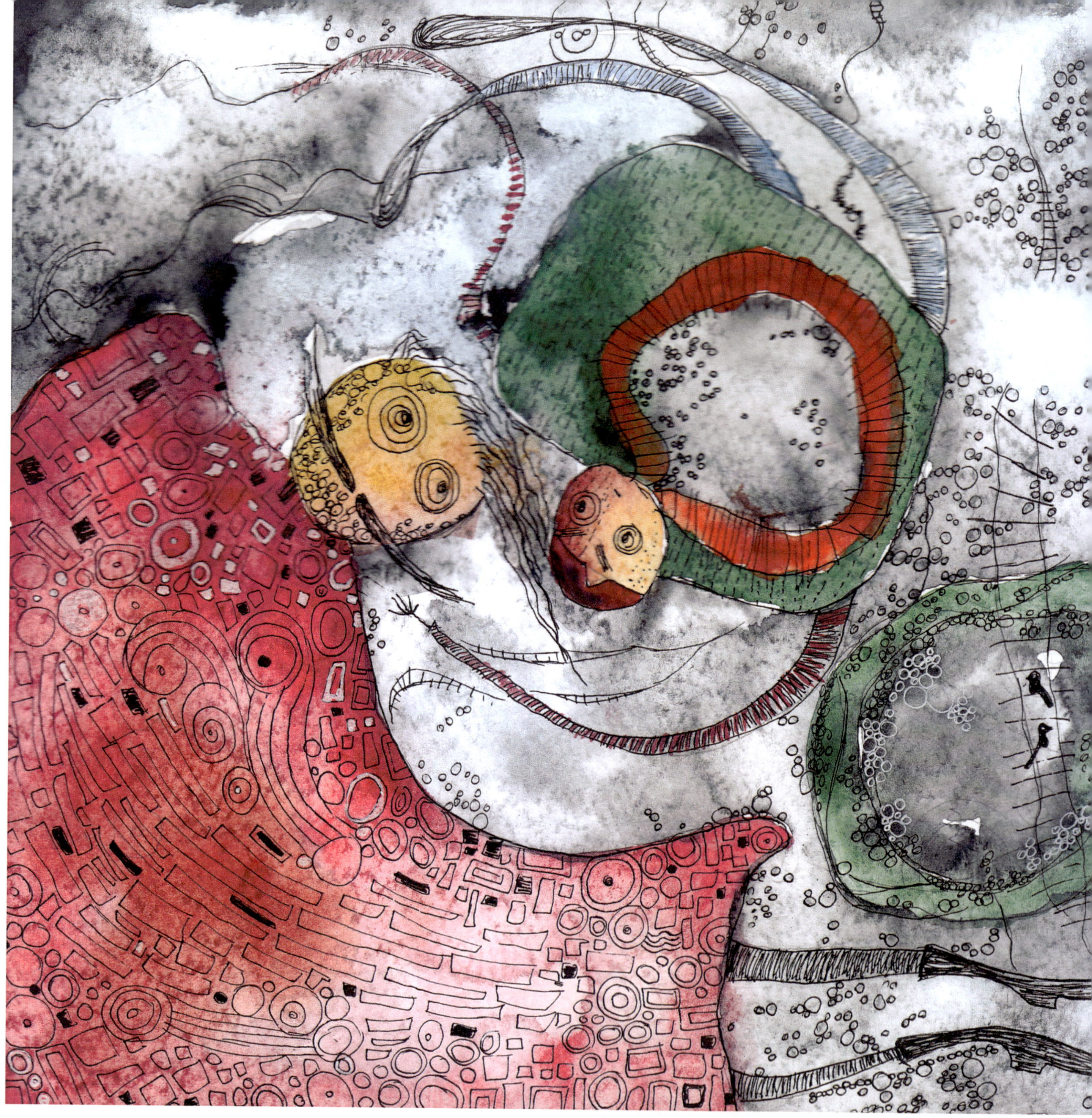

IT WAS HIM. IT WAS ME.

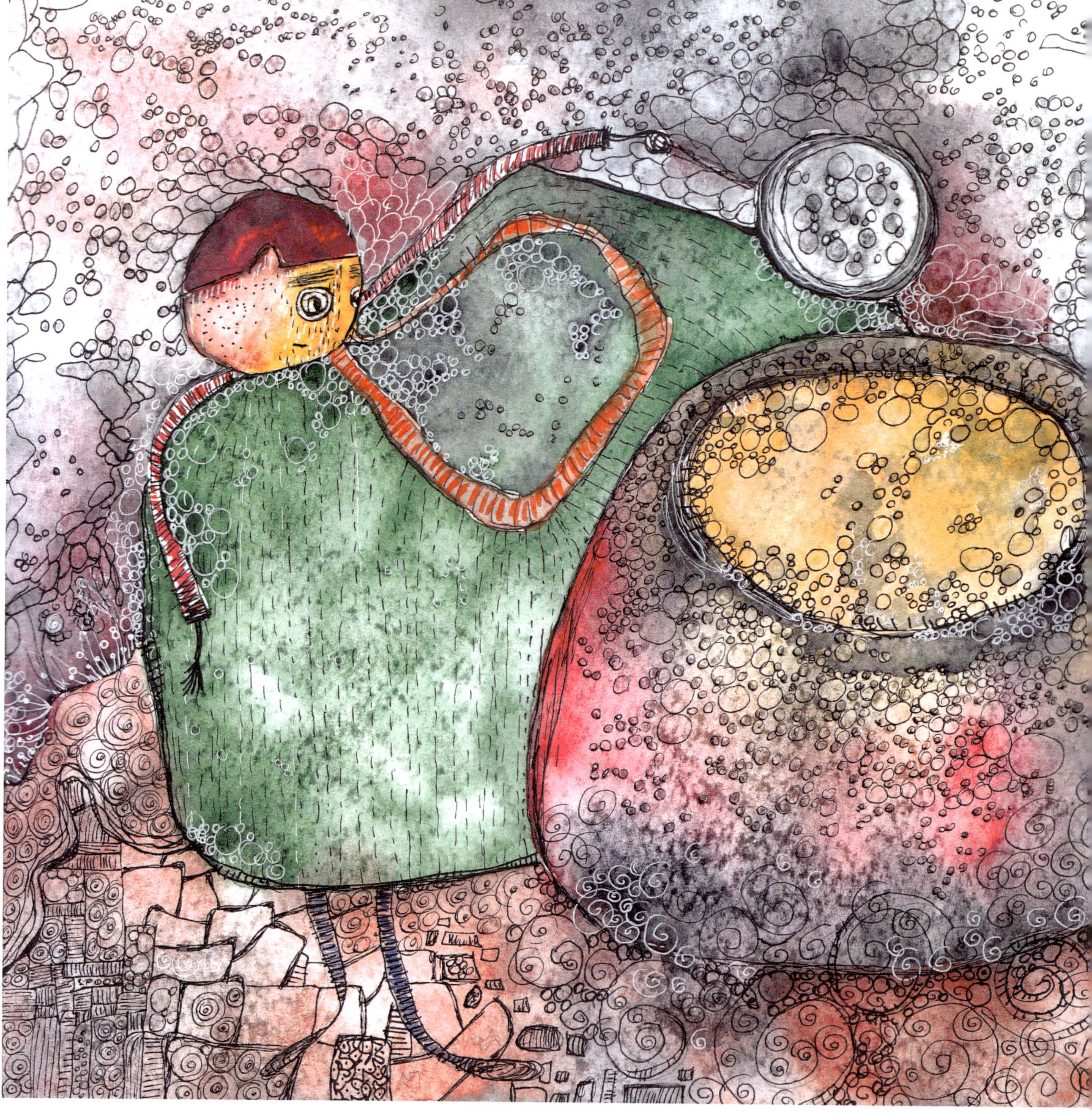

I WAS COOKING.

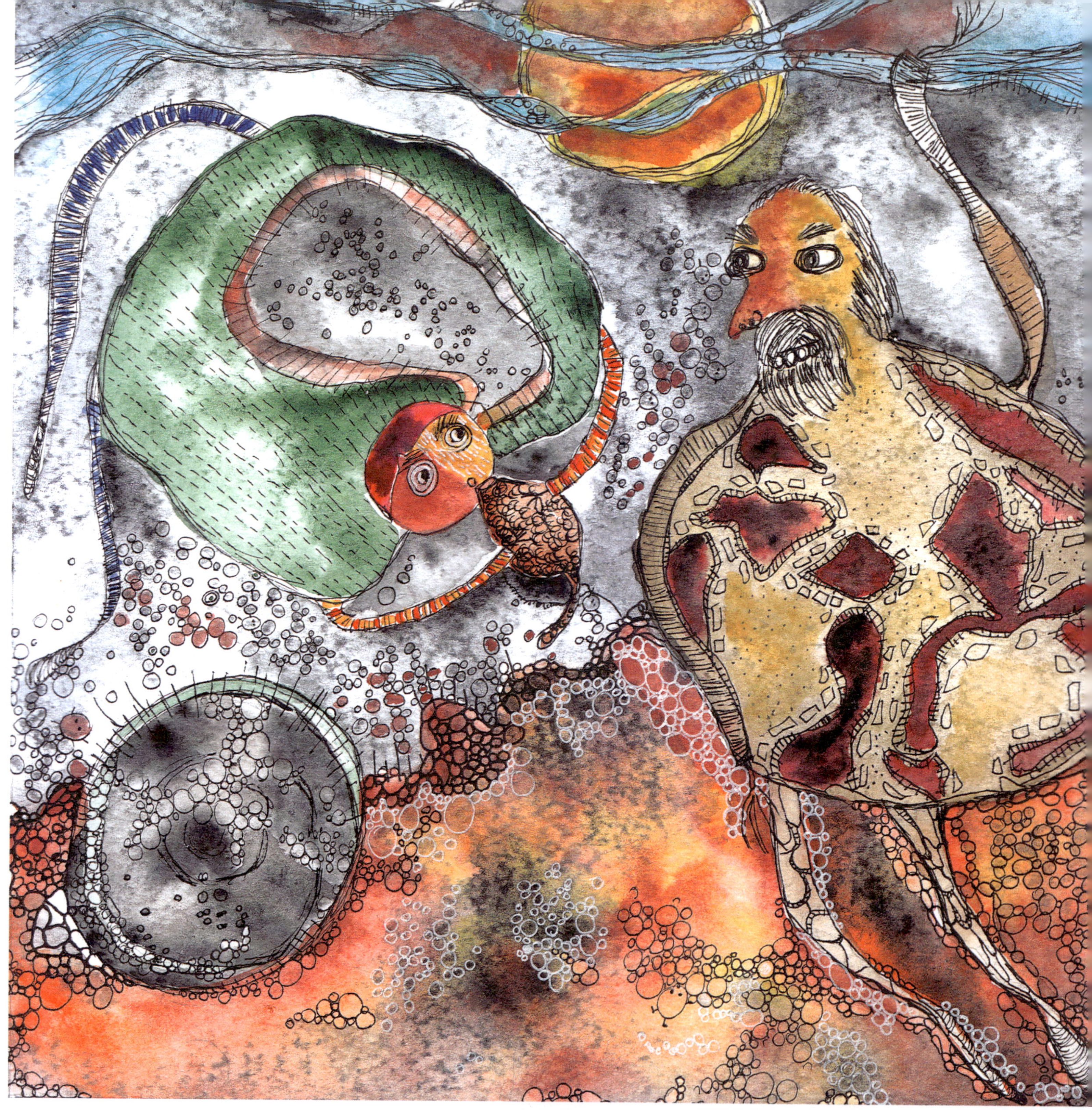

I WAS PLAYING THE BAGPIPES.

I WAS RIDING A HORSE.

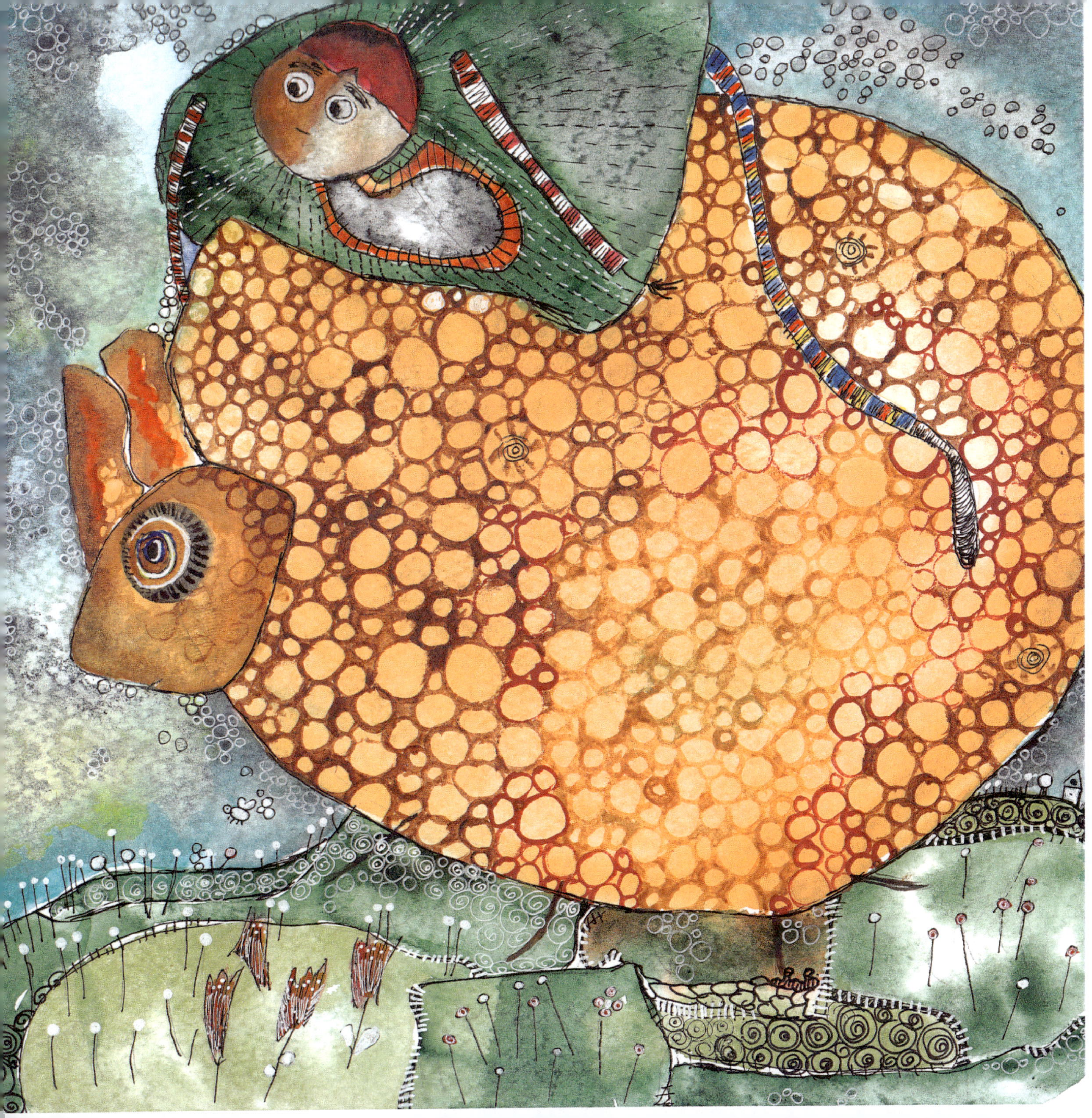

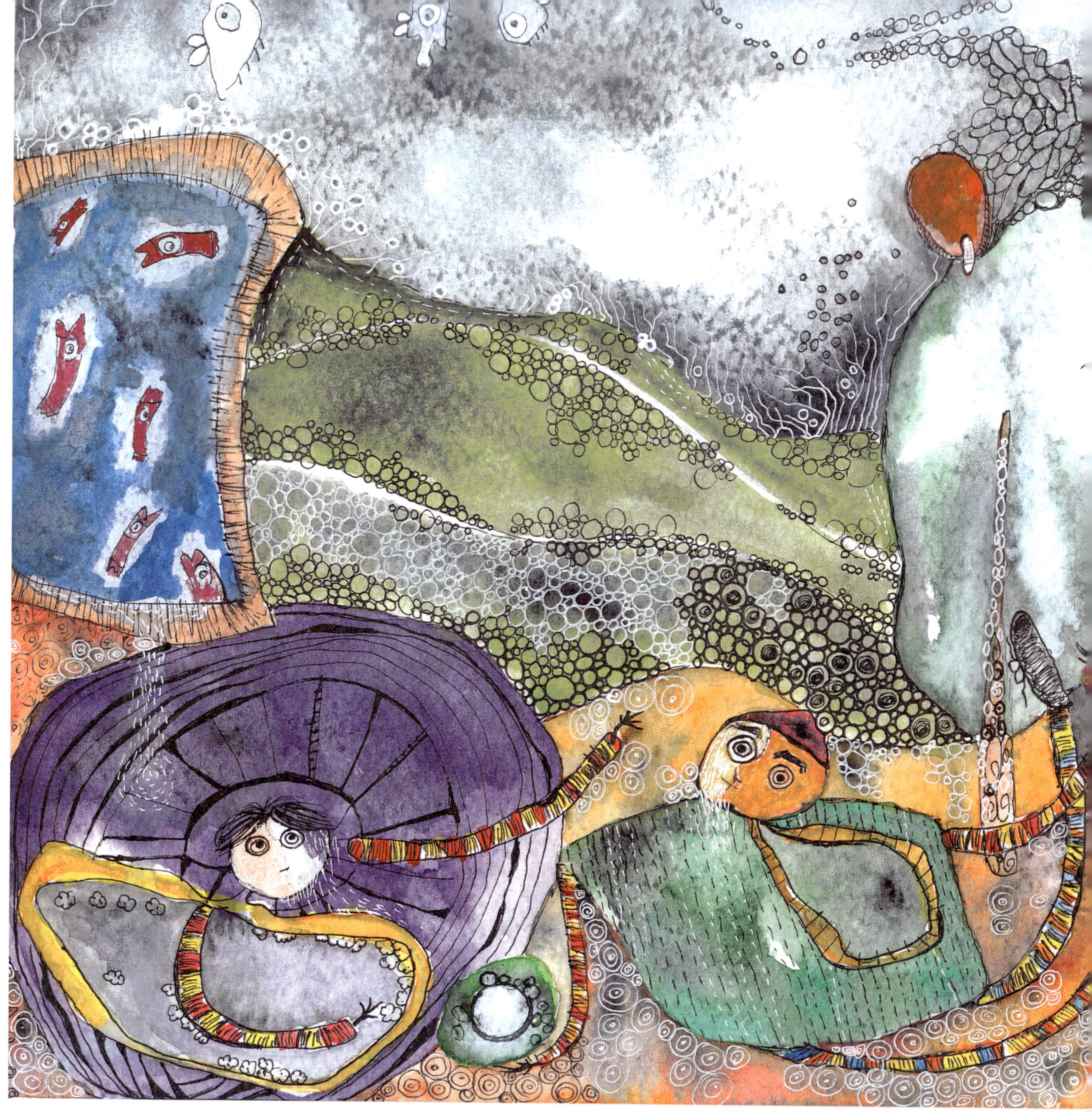

OH NO, WAITE !!!... I AM HERE WITH MY SISTER UNDER THE OLEASTER TREE NOW!

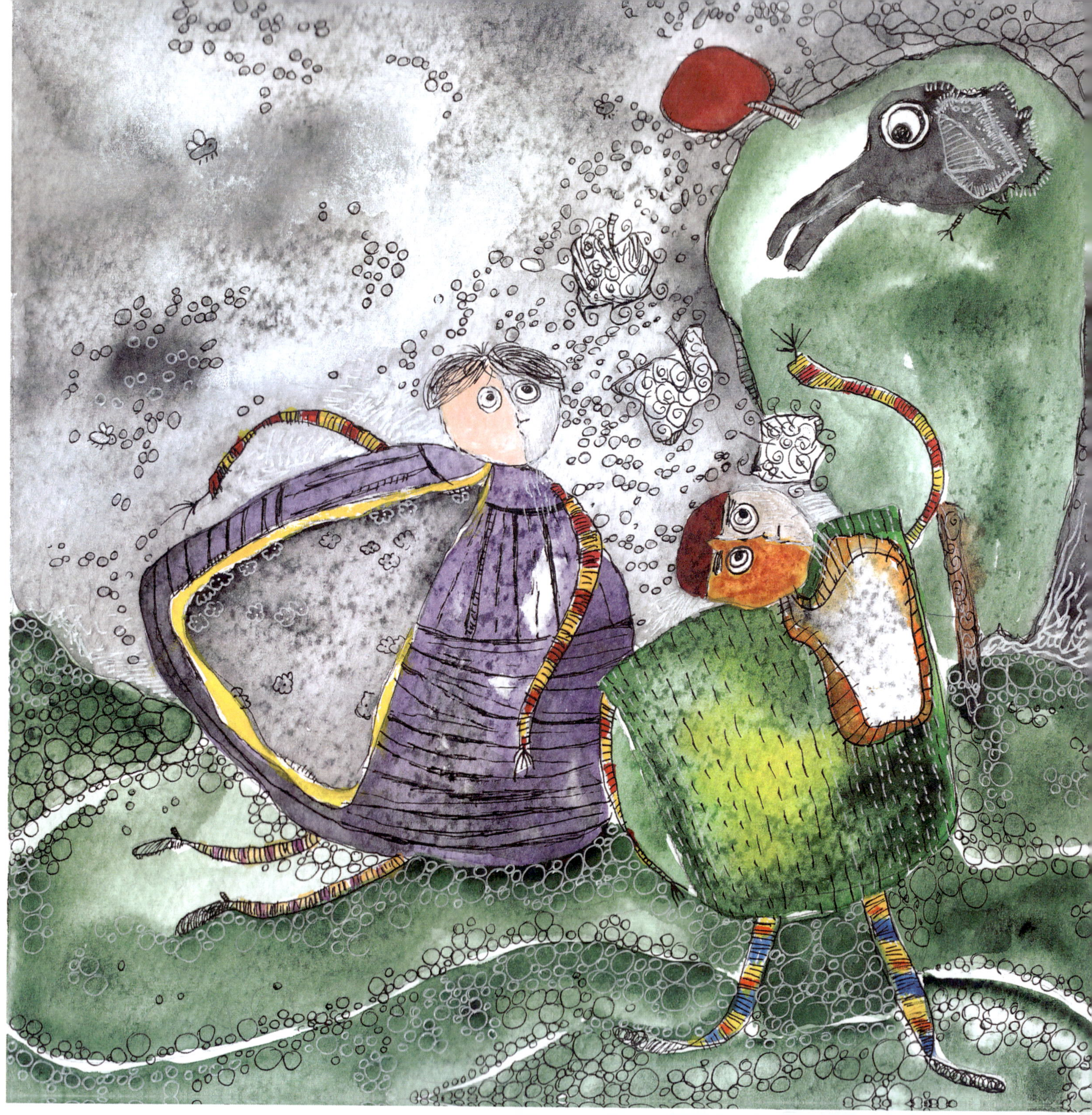

A CROW TOOK THE LAST OLEASTER FROM THE TREE.

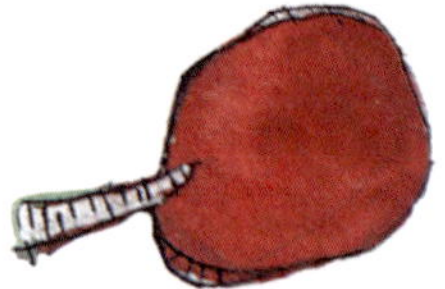

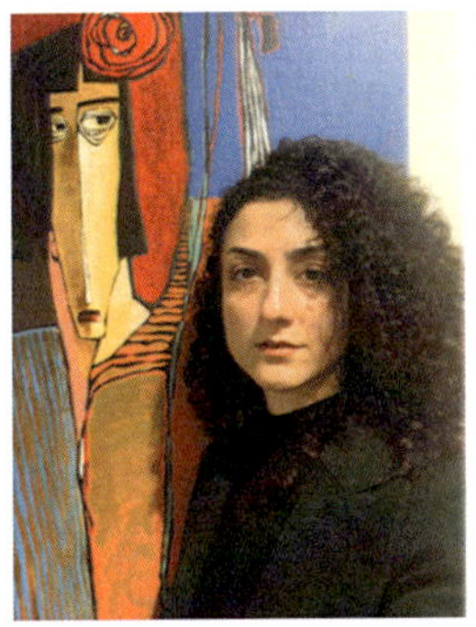

Bahar Taghiani is an illustrator and visual artist whose love for visual imagery began in early childhood. She started by creating characters out of pieces of paper, placing them in imagined stories, and bringing them to life. Today, her artworks are primarily created using mediums such as acrylic, collage, colored pencil, and watercolor, drawing inspiration from her perception of the world around her. Bahar is an award-winning artist, recognized by UNICEF for her illustration in the competition "Children on the Eve of New Year."

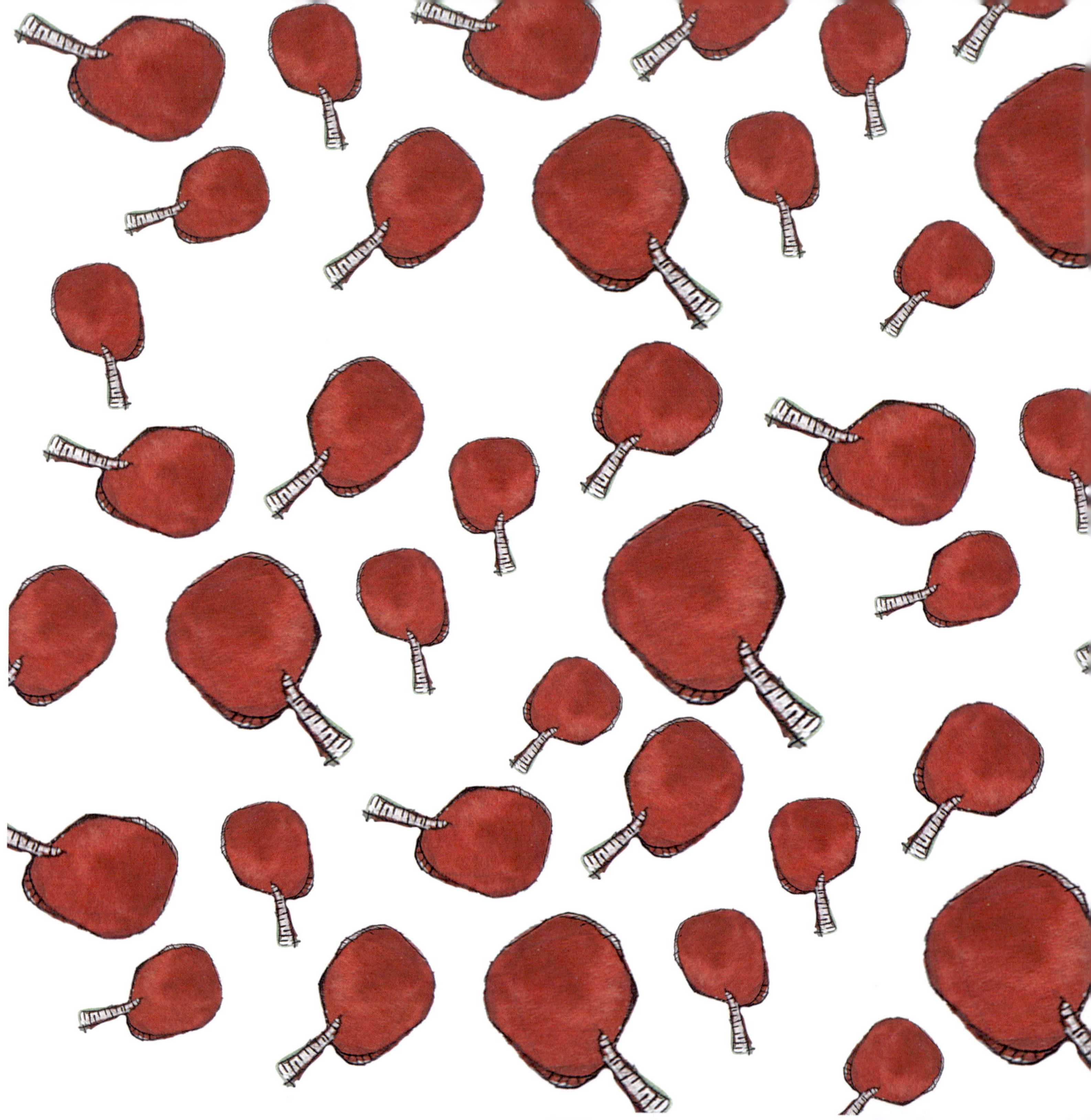

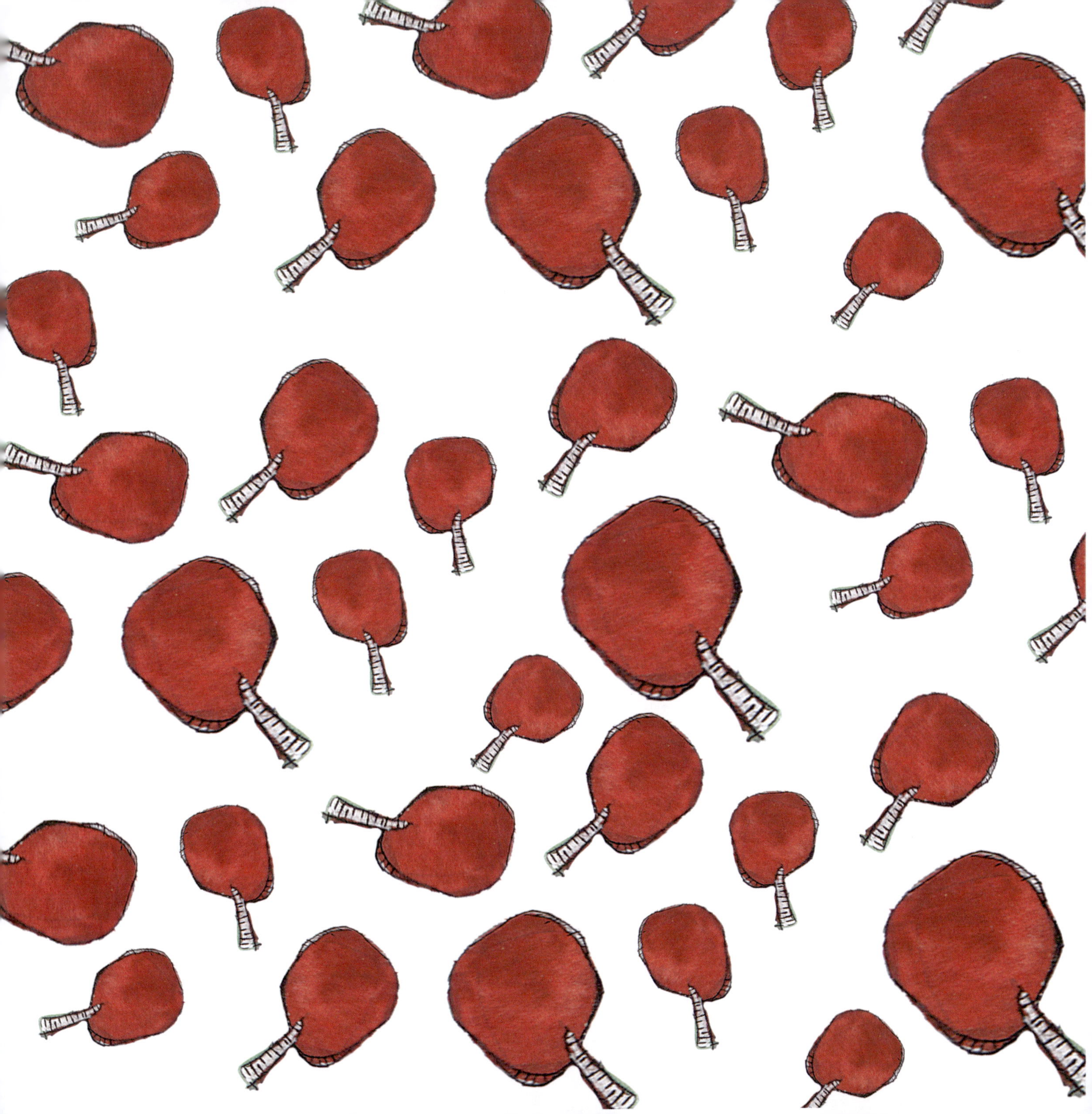

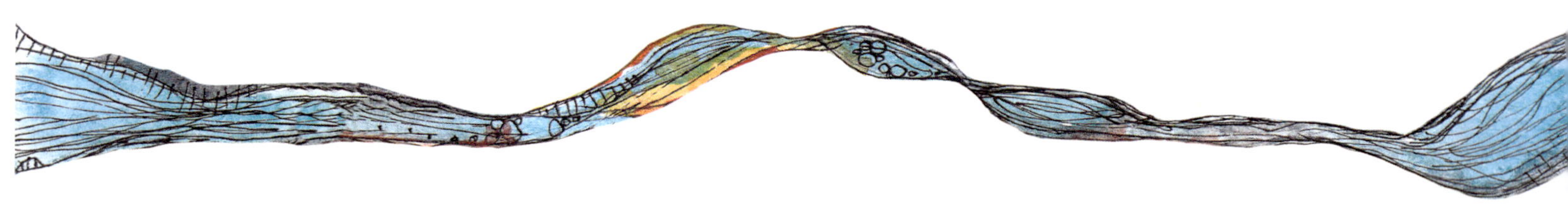

www.ingramcontent.com/pod-product-compliance
Lightning Source LLC
Chambersburg PA
CBRC102023050726
47602CB00013B/167